T0132093

Art in Life

Jeffrey Gale F.R.S.A.

AuthorHouse™ UK
1663 Liberty Drive
Bloomington, IN 47403 USA
www.authorhouse.co.uk
Phone: 0800 047 8203 (Domestic TFN)
+44 1908 723714 (International)

© 2019 Jeffrey Gale F.R.S.A.. All rights reserved.

No part of this book may be reproduced, stored in a retrieval system,
or transmitted by any means without the written permission of the author.

Published by AuthorHouse 08/22/2019

ISBN: 978-1-7283-8247-0 (sc)
ISBN: 978-1-7283-8248-7 (e)

Print information available on the last page.

Any people depicted in stock imagery provided by Getty Images are models,
and such images are being used for illustrative purposes only.
Certain stock imagery © Getty Images.

This book is printed on acid-free paper.

Because of the dynamic nature of the Internet, any web addresses or links contained in this book may have changed
since publication and may no longer be valid. The views expressed in this work are solely those of the author and do not
necessarily reflect the views of the publisher, and the publisher hereby disclaims any responsibility for them.

authorHOUSE®

Contents

Front cover. *<u>**Collioure from hill valley above:**</u> There is a history of famous Artists staying here, like Picasso, Salvador Dali, Braque, Magritte, Max Ernst and C. R. MacKintosh. I made several paintings, land and seascapes while staying with friends nearby. About this period I spent a year in Cadaquès and became friendly with Salvador Dali. Our small trio (flutes, guitar and tablas), played for him in his extraordinary house in Port Ligat. It was an inspiring time for me in Cadaquès as the energies, special light and energised landscape made painting a very mystical experience. With some success in five exhibitions held there, it financially enabled me to continue my planned journey to India, and realising that I could live simply from my paintings. (1979–1980 period).

ART IN LIFE

Most of these poems have specific themes that are actually or metaphorically descriptive of human and wildlife views of this beautiful world. Most were composed specially for our "Poetry and Music" program, held monthly and broadcast on Sound Art Radio studios in Dartington, Totnes, Devon (102.5 FM).

Each program had a special theme to highlight many primary aspects of our lives and other sentient beings on this Planet Earth.

My paintings on covers and inside show places visited during my extensive worldwide travels.

Your feedback appreciation is welcome.
Contact me on tel. 01803 866349 (pref); or jeffrey@worldpeacegardensnet.org

Life is the Mind of this Universe

Nightly I love to walk under the purple vault,
scored by ten thousand million diamonds slowly rotating …
How can I project my being into the mind of this,
our homespun Universe …?

*   *   *

When time is right will mind collapse to free my soul,
into this ultimate so spacious unity,
or can my blind will transport me to another state of being,
to find another home to grow inside?

*   *   *

While walking, face upturned, this is my view into this vasty web,
wondering, will I be guided to oblivion,
or to another voyage across this endless space,
to find the ultimate mystery of life.

*   *   *

One fact is sure, that life itself continues,
it just rotates, as do the Planets round the Sun.
For me there cannot be oblivion, since life renews itself,
and this spectacular arcadia we call Nature,
can herself migrate to many other levels, unknown unseen.
How could this fair earth just slowly die with all its Beings!

*   *   *

Everyone would like to know,
Just what does happen when we go?
Could it be our souls migrate into a mystical place,
And choose to fly into the realms of lightless space.

*   *   *

Though ideas are endless, this one is very clear:-
Our bodies age as do all beings, we may fear to lose
our personality, our sensual pleasures, creative powers, friends,

lovers, and all the beauties of Nature …
Perhaps our greatest fear of all is not to be at all.

*　　*　　*

Considering all, it seems one gets the truest insight
to another life, within the theatre of our dreams,
the door to that vast realm called Consciousness.

*　　*　　*

The Heart of Art is a Mystery

Realising visually in my paintings
strangely beautiful landscapes,
they emerge by some mystical ability
to mix and brush the colours guided by my soul. & mind.

*   *   *

Is it that humans need embrace the mystery in their lives,
just as they do love;
And can I say that art is like the closest child of love,
whose eyes can be as deep and clear as mountain pools;
so this can make my painting like an act of love.

*   *   *

While I wonder through these lanes of life,
there is the hope that I may one day find
the soulful twin of my desires,
whose eyes do signal sparkling recognition.

*   *   *

This much I do know for sure,
that painting is my portal into love,
the golden gift of spiritual consciousness,
whose brush – drawn visions can yield some glimpses into heaven!

*   *   *

Surely the highest art contains a mystery,
that passes through the mind
into the deeper realms of consciousness,
to feed a special kind of transcendent peace.

*   *   *

Currently there is this prevalent idea,
that concepts of the mind
can truly be called works of art;
but if they miss this mystery, they may do
no more than glorify materialism.

*   *   *

The Art of Living

One can try to make one's life into an art.
Certainly if considering all activities as creative acts,
then living itself becomes an art form.
We humans have a very precious role
as spiritually evolved beings in this Universe to be creative.

*　*　*

Critics will surely say,
You can't possibly be creative every moment of the day?
And you may then reply:-
If I can truly make my claim that living is an art,
it's merely down to what one means by Art … ?

*　*　*

For Art is one great mystery …
The greatest works of art can override the rational mind.
Only half of what I do or think is reasonably rational,
the rest is pure imagination or intuition.

*　*　*

You may perceive your life is only mind at work,
but that is very superficial,
much, much more surrounds the life of the soul,
And that must be the greatest mystery of all.

*　*　*

We are all spiritual beings;
the fabric of our bodies is built of spinning balls of energy;
Surely we must be much more than that?
Scientists do now agree that we and all the Universe
are simply made of consciousness.

*　*　*

Like surfers on the sea,
we ride upon the waves of consciousness,
for there's the art, the Art of Living.

*　*　*

Freedom in Art and Life

There are so many ways to be creative.
For me the best is making paintings and architecture …
It's here my freedom lies for ever in the act,
And meditation is my secret key to open doors sublime.

*   *   *

So if you ask me where freedom is?
It's in this act I call creative meditation,
Wherein there is this joy of letting go
the usual chores of body functions.

*   *   *

When merged into the spiritual heart it really feels like flying,
My mind is bless'd to go to any place,
to deepest seas and distant planets,
there is no limit and no barrier.

*   *   *

Most people like that cruising round this world,
to see exotic places will give them freedom.
But without the open gates and soul,
its all illusion, and may too often lead to loneliness.

*   *   *

We humans have the blessing of imagination …
Just like our limbs, this needs to exercise,
Stretching its seemingly limitless possibilities
into those distant fascinating realms as yet unseen.

*   *   *

Surely the best way to be free,
is to open the gates of equipoise,
to find the ultimate truth in soulful quiet meditation.

*   *   *

The Living Art

There is art in Life and there always will be.
One can make everything one does into a kind of art …
but if its boring, one must say this is not art,
And stop doing what must surely be a waste of time!

*   *   *

For there can be art in all one does;
One can perfect the skill of cycling, cleaning, washing up,
to make them into dance, and thus negate the boredom.
Is this just a matter of values or approach?

*   *   *

A conceptualist might say:-
"If I present these objects to the world as Art,
and place them in a Gallery,
where people flock to see them saying,
"This must be art, its in a Gallery!"

*   *   *

Then they go away thinking,
"These objects left me cold in mind and heart,
is there really any art in this?
Or is it just a critics way
of finding something new to say,
in this the present barren field of Art.

*   *   *

Surely it's beauty we all long for,
And beauty is one essential food for soul and mind …
With beauty in our eyes, there's life in our hearts,
and this makes life worth living.

*   *   *

Art is one great mystery …
the greatest work of art can override the rational mind,
setting the soul singing!
If you find any art in this poem,
please let me know, then I'll rejoice!

*   *   *

"The Travelling Mind"

Why Travel my friend when you can go there in your mind,
For there you'll surely find the strangest lands,
mountains on islands hardly visited by Man.
Make friends dear heart, with your imagination,
And there you'll see people and the places,
you cannot find in travel books.

*   *   *

Lay down upon the quiet greensward
Relax into the Natural mind,
And soon you'll let the spirits guide you
through to their most finely coloured world
of luminous green or amber caves,
with pools reflecting gold or indigo light.

*   *   *

One flag I hoist above all others on this day,
that shows a golden circle edged in blue
What means this sign you say?
Quite simply, travel round the circle of your mind
to visit places way beyond the speed of light
Slow down the body, while the mind moves to infinite speeds.

*   *   *

Mind fuelled by consciousness can travel instantly
into the life born planets of some distant galaxy,
Where beings have long since learned the wisdom
of slowing down the body,
and swimming in a sea of consciousness.

*   *   *

We must celebrate this freedom of the travelling mind …
Such gifts must be so rare in this vast universe …
Its just one more aspect of being human,
For this I give my heart felt thanks.

*   *   *

Intro to our Poetry & Music show on Sunday 3rd December 2017

"Hear my friends, lovers of fine poetry, this is the gold and silver of my heart & mind."

The theme of this show is "Winter Spirit."

"Journey of a foraging Falcon over ice-white Dartmoor."

INTRO:

Words and inspirational places in the life of a Peregrine Falcon as he drifts over
Dartmoor from the Dart meet to Dartmouth cliffs, feeling the ancient leyline, his
dark shape hanging over the bleakly pristine moors rising up to rocky lors.

*　　*　　*

Ever vigilant, he scans the land for rabbits, voles, grouse and pigeons; he's seen as one majestic
king of Dartmoor life. His grey back and white speckled front inflect the present mood of Bride like
moor. Stooping on pigeons or Grouse, he dives like a bolted spear on the prey, even as it flies.

*　　*　　*

Lonely as the Moor, by Bentor, Sharp and Hockinston, circling in graceful ease, my widened
wings caress the air, I'm ever watchful for a careless grouse or rabbit down below …
Heh! that flapping bird down there must be my prey …

Gathering my grit, I make one powerful downward thrust, then clap my wings flat,
not falling but diving, I strike the peaceful pigeon, breaking its neck to descend in a fury of feathers …
Oh joy! my hunger is assuaged, as I tear the bird in relish.

*　　*　　*

Feeling restored, I slowly start up to follow my familiar route, south over Holme Moor from Dartmeet …
After circling Bench Tor, swoop to course the Dart a while in the greenly shaded Holme Wood,
then beat again to scan the Pound in Hembury Fort,
where rabbits often feed amongst the lush green grass,
tho' not today where snow lies far too deep.

*　　*　　*

Next I spy the spire of Buckfast Church, part blackened by the fire …
then rotating this I dive again to see the icebound fall

of Riverford Weir, spanned by the ancient Bridge.
Next there may be pigeons perched amongst the trees in gardens of homes in Cott and Swallowfields …
They're wise to hide in branches far too difficult to dive upon.

*   *   *

At length I'm glad to see the snow-bound roofs
of Totnes, gathered round the collared Ness of Castle,
where the noble Mary stands aloof.
While ever sending blessings far and wide;
And like for me today, she is the saving guide
to many a lost and lonely walker on the far horizons of the Moor.

*   *   *

After circling the Town, I'm beating down the Dart
following the edge of Longmarsh,
towards the Sharpham mound, classically crowned
with a stately vista all down the winding River …
Perhaps with luck I'll spot some flocks of Mallards?

*   *   *

The waters lead me on past Gabriels Creek,
opposing, a Heron proudly perched on the White Rock,
from whence I rise serenely over Beacon Hill,
when come the Winter Solstice, the locals build a fire to mark the time …
Then down again in one great swoop, I see the boat by Ferry Quay,
before a gently gliding rise past Higher Farm Tower,
and thence the sea, pounding cliffs by Froward Point …
At last I see my eyrie, where there was the start of this my
noble life, and my noble line.

*   *   *

This journey marks the ancient memory earthbound straight
from Dartmeet down to Froward next to Dartmouth;
And all the points and places seen are markers
For the energetic line, that helps to tell the story
of our beautiful home; but like the Falcon,
only a base for fine adventures far and wide.

*   *   *

Love in a Freezing Winter

There is no love,
without the pulsing rhythm of your heart,
And only you can resonate with mine,
this steady beat within, is now our common source.

*   *   *

There is no life,
without the quickening pulsing rhythm of our hearts,
as when we meet there comes a warmth inside,
that we must feel as simple as magic mixed with bliss.

*   *   *

I need this love,
when winter storms with freezing gales
can bend the whispering Pines outside,
and sweep the mounting snow off roofs.

*   *   *

So surely I do need your love,
to share this flaming fire inside,
and wrap a rug around our mutual warmth,
to keep at bay this raging storm outside.

*   *   *

Like me, you must have need to share your love,
and come within my cosy house to hear fine music,
while we kiss away our sensual desire,
and learn again our bliss of unity.

*   *   *

Our Portal of Dreamland

This you may dispute, but do believe my saying,
your dreams can be a portal to another plane,
a mystic world so very different, yet oddly familiar
as if on drifting into sleep
there is a dream – trees, inviting you to climb into a paradise realm.

*   *   *

Since childhood the old oak trees have challenged me
to climb their twisting boughs, to sit up there alone
to dream, and let the unconscious actors
step outside the greenly veiled proscenium.

*   *   *

They clearly aren't concerned about our lives,
Just carry on acting their fascinating scenes in curious ways,
Although they sometimes seem to send me friendly smiles
we cannot wish to break the silken veil between us.

*   *   *

Though glad to find this other world, we wonder
could it just be our minds way of enjoying its hidden freedoms,
Or a portal to another realm,
populated by extraordinary people in extraordinary places.

*   *   *

My life like yours must have its secret outlets,
while gazing at a sparkling fountain,
or a multi-coloured flaming fire,
we love to fuel our inner dreams,
and watch our minds crossing all the usual frontiers.

*   *   *

The Breathing Sea

Do you love to breathe with the sea?
Revive some ancient memories within,
asleep in the swell and fall of intimate waters,
quietly moving in the bladderack of briny air.
*   *   *

While walking by the sea,
its all in me to let emerge these strange longings,
to see them in the sparkling dance across the waves,
and in the steady swell and fall of wayward tides,
there is this lung of truth inside ourselves.
*   *   *

Just like you and me the sea has moods;
while now she sleeps this blissful hours serene,
there'll be a time not far away,
when innocent rippling's will change to crashing foam!
*   *   *

In you, in me the change will come,
startling like a rising tempest churned within,
we must fight to calm our problematic minds,
or let these problems fall away when sun beams out,
and peace returns to shine on grateful waves.
*   *   *

Must we go down to the sea to meet ourselves?
For there must be the seeds of all our lives
that like our moods will change each day
from deep azure, to green then grey.
*   *   *

Deep down we know she has it all this sea …
she loves the moon and rises when she's full
Is this the whim of gravity held into elliptical paths,
or yet another mystery of consciousness that we are part.
Meanwhile, let's all breathe deeply by the sea.
*   *   *

Breath of Life

The day the plants and trees do breathe again,
they love the sun and draw down deep,
to suck the sap to make a magic alchemy with air and sun,
creating a kind of music in such colours
that you or I can dream on.

*   *   *

If life is breath then may I walk with trees
and flowers down a scented way,
to join this breathing chorus from plant to plant, tree to tree,
to sing their songs, while Blackbirds break the air!

*   *   *

Now I wonder how they do transform such rainbow colours
into such rapturous songs our best Composers find so marvellous,
and yet find much too variable to mimic.

*   *   *

Hear their songs to know how Nature holds
such secrets of creation, so bold to leave our minds
not blank, but thirsty for her sounds and scents,
to make a poem or painting not wanting in its beauty.

*   *   *

Our alchemy of transformation can build from tiny sparks,
while taking deeper breaths, can whip them into flames,
and from these secrets thoughts or moods we make
the forms and colours of our paintings, poems and stories.

*   *   *

May mind and heart join forces with my soul,
to forge the shape, rhythm or colour of this poem,
being itself a hyme of thankfulness
to all the living, moving, exuberant scenes this Nature has to give,
let me embrace you as the lover that you are.

*   *   *

My Voice is my Instrument

How I love to sing!
For in singing I can improvise freely,
something not so easy in the spoken word,
Except perhaps in free-form poetry?

*   *   *

Usually I feel elated when singing,
as the deep breathing fills my heart with oxygen,
and my mind with joyful creativity in words
in voice transformed to music.

*   *   *

One reflects that down the ages,
Chanting has always been the way to share with God
our praise and feelings in great Monasteries, Churches
and Cathedrals, beautifully built to resonate their songs.

*   *   *

While vocalising I can breathe deeply to remember who I am,
a breathe, a throat, a lung, a mind
at once in harmony, in resonance;
what joy to find this unity within.

*   *   *

Walking in this woodland on a windy day,
the trees do make their whispering songs like symphonies
to soothe the soul …
Another day I rush to seek their shelter from a storm,
and love to hear the swishing howls, creaking, crackling
roars these dancing trees can make,
loving the cleansing gale, finding another kind
of dynamic life, transcending their usual greenly
tranquil states.
I'll join their chorus with my song inside.
My name Gale, this first time used – birds in flight, sailing, storms, winds fascinate me.

*   *   *

Global Warming – Crisis or Salvation?

This world of ours is changing fast,
the time to save it's come, and past says lovelock,
so let'd build nuclear and coal-fired plants,
then all us Northerners can live the same old way,
Buying and flying, binging and borrowing,
until we reach that fateful day
When world turns round and comes to say –
I'll burn and flood you all away,
You pestilential people, you'll never learn
that I'm the one upon, you finally depend!

*   *   *

Your techno fire may temporary save,
But when my floods come raging down,
It's sad to say that they, like you will drown.
But then you say, we'll build our boats,
And sail away to the high hills,
To plant our gardens, come what may,
A cosy little shack you see, no frills!
These folk are lucky so you say,
But no, it's just they've learnt the skills,
And sceptically prepared themselves for this,
the time to change our ways not then, but right away.

*   *   *

So – let's throw away our oil & plasticized existence,
And plant our food productive trees & gardens,
Make compost & electricity in small scale digester plants,
Water and wind turbine, with panels on our roofs
Will give us all the power we need.
In these co-operative creeds, we'll all stand proud
to sow our seeds into the generous and loving earth.

*   *   *

This painting shows my project for Cosmic Eco-Homes suggested for a small site behind Schumacher College, Dartington Hall Estate, near Totnes, Devon, England. The 2-storey homes are based on the Natural Geometry of 3. On the ground floor 3 earth block circular rooms are oversailed by hexagonal timber-framed bedrooms. The bridging units between them contain kitchen-diner with bathroom or gallery over. The bathroom roofs are covered entirely in PV solar panels. The 3 circles exactly face South to maximise solar gain, enclosing a private walled garden. Originally in 1976 I proposed a Hamlet Community of 12 of these Eco-homes on a site above Warren Lane, near the ancient Hall itself, with support of Maurice Ash, the Chairman of the Dartington Hall Trust at the time. A model was made of the eco-home and exhibited in Higher Close near the site, along with a layout of 12 homes facing a stepped earth ampitheatre.

Although this project was widely praised by staff and students of the Dartington Arts College, who were to be housed, along with six for self-build highly skilled building team, the majority of Trustees would not vote for it. This was my second attempt to initiate a Hamlet, the first being in central Exeter, with similar houses of self-built design. The site owners, a Charitable Trust, preferred to sell to a local spec builder. Feeling disillusioned with English capitalism, I left in 1979 to begin my slow journey to India.

"Our Union is Divine"

Dear love, you hold my flame in your caressing hand,
While we do plunge so slowly down the deep embracing pool
of oneness.
Gliding in this buoyant clarity, we are at last one soul
beyond this time or place have entered space inhabited by Angels;
*   *   *

We rise into each others warmth,
Sliding through the snows of Belovodya,
while every sorrow and frustration slips away.
This timeless time, we know we're much much more
than mind or memory,
Just spirits longing for our union,
And just, through deepest, highest, purist love,
have both encountered Heaven.
*   *   *

Let's float for ever in this turquoise crystal depth,
transcending body's hot insistence,
into white, and many coloured hues of primal wisdom.
*   *   *

Dearest one, from your eyes ecstatic joy
I see the face of God,
Whose pure delight is sharing all Creation
in this, our one eternal moment …..
*   *   *

Source light and life so we recalled, when two perfected spheres
Did merge to birth these eyes, expressive portals of one soul,
too soon have lost, then spent those worldly years
in search for this, our union.
*   *   *

Dear reader, who can ever hope
to let you see or feel what this is like,
Except to say through purist love exchanged, this window opens wide
to glimpse a vista quite beyond our earthly paradise.

*   *   *

In Cornworthy

Strolling up the lane by crowding cottages, lights from windows,
and past the sombre church tower,
I turned by a high stone wall into level mall,
To greet the wide sweeps of the evening sky,
where silvered ice islands subtly change their shape & hue
by the second in the luminous blue,

*   *   *

A time-speed mirror of our slowly moving island,
set in the shimmering oceans.
This upside down universe carries my spirit
through my body-rocking patchwork golds and greens,
so sensually locked languidly to the mist-grey,
tight-lipped moons, crouching under the vast sky.

*   *   *

Exhalant, my spirit swims into this metamorphic sea …
Time has fled, I'm here where I belong,
the island sailor freed by my visions,
Yet bound by ever changing Destiny.

*   *   *

Ode to Fowey

Is there a poet here today
With thoughts of Fowey?
Who couldn't feel some memories
of joy filled times
and deepening vistas there.

*   *   *

My friends who live there
high upon the hill,
enjoy the view across Fowey Creek …
In the azure sits an amphitheatre
of tottering towers and pubs,
the perfect stage for wondering minstrels,
or spontaneous street singers,
and for a drama waiting now to happen.

*   *   *

One wonders what became of fisher folk,
and brave seamen fending off
marauding French pirates.
When a smaller Fowey remembered King Mark,
and the welcome landing of the Princess Isolde,
into the loving arms of Tristan.

*   *   *

When there I pleased to feed my mind,
from whispering Cedars towering up the hill,
and wanderings in narrow lanes,
gyrating in a complex dance
around the tall forbidding Church.

*   *   *

And there in Place upon the hill,
my friends breathe in the vista,
and breathe out their stories & their poems
across the world, floating out to land in resonant minds.

*   *   *

This becomes a tribute to my friends,
with many happy memories
of Solstices and other celebrations …
It's gratitude I feel,
for friendship over decades, that must remain.

*   *   *

A special Cornish Poetry evening was held
at Sharpham House, organised by Alice Oswald,
a well known local poet who runs these
monthly Poets Circle meetings. This one I wrote
specially for this occasion,
and several Cornish Poets were invited. (*nr Totnes)

*   *   *

For Andy, a Man who loves trees

In the forest where you live,
every tree is an all-giving tree,
every bush and herb has life – giving fragrance,
every stone is a philosophers stone.

*   *   *

And this space on Earth is a Pilgrims holy place,
Having water's nectar against ageing …
Here they sing their golden songs,
these birds are sacred,
you're bless'd to share their simple fare.

*   *   *

And if you stumble on a stone,
it is a wishing crystal with powers to serve your every need.
Lord, what do you desire, when all is here provided,
Your presence is all around,
when consciousness is open to perceive.

*   *   *

A poem inspired by one great mystic of Indian the 12th cent.
Mahadevi – yakka. She spent large parts
of her short life in the forests of Mysore
as a wondering poet without possessions.
Her originals were in Kannada, similar to Sanskrit.

*   *   *

Spring Storm

Now one feels the wild wind-like beast
that's longing to escape,
hurling itself against this shuttered house
with such ferocity, I fear to breach my door …
Still, this is life, a need to step outside
my cosy boundaries into this fearful fray,
though the gale slaps my face,
she whips my cap away,
this cold stimulation starts a rigor in my mind
that too much sloth has dulled.

*   *   *

Bent low to cut the storm,
she tears my clothes and draws my cloak
high into the roaring air, swirling and flying up,
just loving a new-found freedom.

*   *   *

Mindfully, I wonder how the sea can be in such a storm,
so, turning, let this wind thrust me down the hill
to see the spray pounding up the cliffs in demented fury
while breathless, my mind responds profoundly
to this glorious gale, and if the stream allows,
I'll fight my weaving way back home,
to flop by fire and write a poem.

*   *   *

Earth's mantle has ways of snatching you up
to shake you like a rag-doll,
sometimes a blessing, sometimes disaster, always a thrill;
the unpredictability of life is what I love, you too?

*   *   *

Harmony Within

At times, when you feel a kind of deep peace within,
then hold it close if you can,
For this is the truth of who you are,
manifest as your redeeming golden guide.

*   *   *

The rock-bed of being truly human
can emerge in quiet places,
like the woodland, lakeside or high hill …
and even sometimes in the temple

*   *   *

There is a certain shining light within
that silently speaks …
No need to travel far and wide
to find your inner harmony:

*   *   *

For its always there waiting quietly,
waiting for you to pierce the mask
of mind protection …
All you need to do is nothing,
Send mind to bed, relax,
and enter the cool caves of enlightenment.

*   *   *

There is no place more worth a visit,
than this your own true self …
Once found, take a walk by the reflective River
for this is the River that connects you to
the Ocean of Consciousness.

*   *   *

The Enigma of Freedom

The relatively of freedom is enormous,
Our nightly sleep must be the great saviour,
A portal of freedom open to us all
For in sleep we can wander, travel far and wide,
visit places and people we've never seen before.
*   *   *

The good Planet turns to give us day & night,
she breathes as we do, inward at the night and outward in the day
How dreadful it must be in Countries by the Pole
where night is scarce, and light prevails.
*   *   *

Those Icelandic people still must have their sleep
for without it they would soon become deranged,
or even die, and this circadian rhythm, is part of our beings
and every function of our body
and most, not all, the functions of our mind.
*   *   *

Perhaps the brain needs more rest than spirit.
Is spirit the choreographer of dreams?
One cannot hold they come from memories alone,
Tho these may play a part
*   *   *

Today we British have more freedom to roam the world
than other generations, not just air flight makes this possible
while our universal language allows communication with most,
and then our entry to such far out lands is rarely blocked.
*   *   *

All races of this world do long for freedom,
to migrate when civil conflict makes the normal life a memory,
when fear haunts the mind, who can find the peace it craves?
This black ghost of fear denies our peaceful dreams,
Even does restrict the freedom of our movement …
If you're blessed with freedom in your mind,
then you have real freedom.
*   *   *

The Heart of Art is a Mystery

Realising visually in my paintings
strangely beautiful landscapes,
they emerge by some mystical ability
to mix and brush the colours guided by my soul.

*　　*　　*

Is it that humans need embrace the mystery in their lives,
as they do love;
And I can say that art is like the closest child of love,
whose eyes can be as deep and clear as mountain pools,
so this can make my painting like an act of love.

*　　*　　*

While I wonder through these lanes of life,
there is the hope that I may one day find
the soulful twin of my desires,
whose eyes do signal sparkling recognition.

*　　*　　*

This much there is I know for sure,
that painting is my portal into love;
the golden gift of spiritual consciousness,
whose brush-drawn visions can yield some glimpses into heaven!

*　　*　　*

There is another aspect of my work,
that always seems to show itself
while sitting meditating on the ground,
the earthly spirit speaks in deeper me,
to guide my brush in hand from mixer to the board.

*　　*　　*

So here again I need to say,
from all my years of painting far and wide,
that art is still the mystical event for which I'm bless'd,
to sit out there to divinate the latent beauties of this Planet Earth.

*　　*　　*

Forgetting to Remember

You must agree its hard to forget sometimes,
experiences, or events one hopes to fall away
keep reappearing, even when one tries forgetting …
Peace and happiness can only be yours when one can
deeply enjoy the now
by forgetting to remember past unhappy experience
and not always looking forward to some future event
or experience.

*   *   *

The art of enjoying now is the art of happiness:
"How beautiful is life, but it flies from us;
if you want to be happy, be happy now
there is no certainty of tomorrow"
I find walking in the woodland and by the streams and Rivers
is a wonderful way to become one with the beauty
of surroundings, their energies, their colours and scents.
Why is nature always so beautiful? in our eyes?
Surely its because she's surrounded us since first
we gathered food, hunted & built shelters
more than 500 years ago.

*   *   *

Hardly surprising how we need to enjoy
and appreciate her woodlands, hills, waters, winds, sounds,
colours, aromas to feel truly contented …
Over this vastly wondrous world I have walked, cycled
and flown, and seen in 500 thousand nows,
how this beauty can become inflected in the whole of me,
so I can now forget to remember, as it's all stored inside.

*   *   *

Warm Heart in a Freezing Body

The thought of you just keeps my heart so warm,
while now I step outside my door
into the deeply snow sealed ice,
swept clean by this Siberian Storm,
clutching my cold hands inside my Russian coat.

*   *   *

Crunching the familiar path towards the lit-up shop,
thinking of your eyes in friendly smile,
while walking in the Tyga Forest,
where sunbeams shafting through the greening canopy,
have made a scintillating carpet reflected in your eyes.

*   *   *

She leads me to a tree lined lake
where whispering Cedars all mirrored in their stately splendour,
are floating there beyond a tree filled island
that beckons its exotic mysteries …

*   *   *

We're urged to shed our clothes,
and breaking peace a little,
quickly find ourselves plunging out between the water lilies,
to swim sensually towards this island,
finding a tiny beach at length,
we land there, flopping down like seals,
to feel the warm sun on our skins.

*   *   *

So now we're relishing the moment,
If ever Heaven comes to bless us,
it must be just like this,
we surely must remember, this peaceful place in time,
and wish it could extend for ever.

*   *   *

Space, Time & Consciousness

In ancient garden where I sit reflecting
how this natural peace is never silent,
the vibrant fiery colours just like flames
are dancing on the whole idea of time …
What is this they say? – we're moving in our circle,
Just the way we always do and always will.

*   *   *

You have no need to think or fret about your ultimate demise,
the invitation comes from Mother Nature and from Father time
to join this, the endless circles of dance in days,
And dreams in nights,
For here must be the so eternal moment,
where time dissolves revealing all that ever was,
And ever will be.

*   *   *

Source of endless inspirations, my deepest well of being
has all the powers of wisdom without limits.
How blessed are human kind who can so easily
just swim the cosmic sea of consciousness,
inside the confines of the soul,
where God awaits to hold you in a warm embrace.

*   *   *

Today the symphony of sounds around me
has the back drop roar of wind shaking a million needles
in the mighty Pines and Cedars.
Experimental time is personally variable.
The mind has powers to bend it, but not as yet create it.
Thoughts, times and messages are sent thru' any barriers of time or space.

*   *   *

Migration to Freedom

Come Spring this pair of Swallows feel the urge
to fly away to the North from torpid African climes,
to the cooler March risings of our Devon Ccoast . . .
where their sweet warbles fill the sky with promise . . .

*   *   *

Like then I feel the enrgy rising,
as the frigid winter days begin to show
small patchy blues between the clouds,
while my mood changes as the skies make room for sunshine.

*   *   *

And with this reborn air comes forked streaks of blue & gold,
their ethereal shimmering warbling makes a counterpoint
with a widely glowing misty sky,
astonished, raising my eyes, seeing their freedom,
there is this restless urge to ascend with them!

*   *   *

Once more I do resolve to fly above the mist,
if not as a bird then in my mind
where ultimate freedom lies.
Let me loose my ties of habitual thoughts,
spiralling aloft to join these swooping swallows.

*   *   *

Their songs of freedom,
can fill an empty soul with hope . . .
But then you question:
"What must I do to justify this freedom?
The answer cries to me right here:
be creative, write poems and make paintings,
for these are my songs of freedom!

*   *   *

Breath of Life

This day the plants and trees do breathe again,
they love the sun and draw down deep,
to suck the sap to make a magic alchemy with air and sun,
creating a kind of music in such colours
that you or I can dream on.

*   *   *

If life is breath then may I walk with trees
and flowers down a scented way,
to join this breathing chorus from plant to plant, tree to tree,
to sing their songs, while Blackbirds break the air!

*   *   *

Now I wonder how they do transform such rainbow colours
into such rapturous songs our best Composers find so marvelous,
and yet find much too variable to mimic.
Hear their songs to know how Nature holds
such secrets of creation, so bold to leave our minds
not blank, but thirsty for her sounds & scents,
to make a poem or painting not wanting in its beauty.

*   *   *

Our alchemy of transformation can build from tiny sparks,
while taking deeper breaths, can whip them into flames,
and from these secret thoughts or moods we make
the forms and colours of our paintings, poems and stories.

*   *   *

May mind and heart join forces with my soul,
to forge the shape, rhythm or colour of this poem,
being itself a hyme of thankfulness
to all the living, moving, exuberant scenes this Nature has to give.
Let me embrace you as the lover that you are.

*   *   *

Fire & *Water*

These days there's fire in my heart
and water in my soul.
By some subliminal accord they don't conflict.
Instead they seem to complement each other
in a kind of corporeal soft diplomacy.

*   *   *

This water has the blessed quality of eating fire,
so when it feels the battle flames arising,
looks on with quiet assurance,
like the sage under a Peeple Tree,
saying, you think you're free,
but in reality you'll self destruct when I come by
to eat you up, you'll see!

*   *   *

Of all the elements of this good Earth,
water is the peace maker,
the eternal giver of all life.

*   *   *

It just takes the passion of my heart and turns it into love.
& with encouragement, can send it round the world
the ultimate balm where fiery battles rage,
dear water always tries to quench the flames.

*   *   *

Meanwhile, I do reflect there is the passionate fire
in men's hearts and minds that must eventually learn
from soul that flames are only good,
when gathered into inspirational love.

*   *   *

The fire that makes the home a home,
can also make a battle ground for some,
tho' far away, their cries can come,
like desperate messengers across the crowded airways.
Always in readiness, the Water Goddess stands on guard since this old world began.

*   *   *

It's Cracking this Fracking

It's cracking this fracking we're starting to hear,
lets add our voices to those far and near,
who value our land above all to be clear
of rashes of towers polluting our air & waters so dear.

*   *   *

We'll fight these frack monsters all of the way,
till short sighted Government,
can start to see the folly of its way,
and ban the hideous Frackers without further delays!

*   *   *

Let's all take our cue,
from our dear neighbours, Scotland, Wales and Eire,
who came out on the side of their people,
to ban these alien frackers forth with . . .

*   *   *

Lets stand up together and sweep them away,
these unwanted wreckers of our precious land,
instead we'll demand more cash to green sources,
with simple and sensible ways we must make our demands.

*   *   *

Remember the young who deserve a clean future,
remember that oil will bring in more plastics,
invading our rivers, our oceans and airs.
It's time to put our cap or Fracks,
to resist them now before it's too late!

*   *   *

People of England, raise up your hands,
to save our lovely lands with our sweeping solidarity!

*   *   *

Considerations of Time

Who knows what time is?
Ask the God who first cast this Planet
into space, with a cricketers twist,
to spin for ever, making night and day.

*   *   *

This spin measures our daily rations of light;
sunlight our great life giver,
all the teeming forms, the birds, insects, animals,
plants, fishes and ourselves do thrive or die rotating, in their time.

*   *   *

Every being feels this inboard timing spin,
and knows what time it is.
We humans have our clocks,
to pace and space our lives; but wait . . .

*   *   *

The Anbean Tribe of isolated Hogy
has banned the use of clocks, watches, or any time device
they see as tools of rampant materialistic societies;
also Banks with their promissory notes of currency are banned.

*   *   *

They view these things as barriers to compassion,
love and the natural sharing of food, shelter, building, skills,
as ways to exchange their assets,
thus avoiding human failings of personal greed and competition.

*   *   *

We all have personal perceptions of passages of time
molded by emotions, travel, events, anticipation,
even trauma, accidents, shocks, drugs,
can each completely change our temporal perception.

*   *   *

Is time merely perception of change?
Even plants know this,
and birds, trouts, penguins, nomads,
know when their time has come to migrate;
babies know their time to be born.

*   *   *

Mind Travel

What is the fastest way to travel to earth?
We may not use it, but we humans can fly to distant places
within the power of our minds and our imaginations.

* * *

You may ask, how can I travel to places never seen?
If you remember even the smallest part of any dream,
it's sure to find you or others in a strange scene,
a distant land you're sure you've never been.

* * *

We restless human souls that are for ever curious,
Will always long to visit strange exciting places way beyond the far horizons …
Surely one of the greatest gifts to humanity is that of seeing
beyond the confines of the brain, outside it's usual functions.

* * *

Even the mindful mind can sometimes feel frustrated,
too imprisoned in the confines of its own routines,
it longs to travel into spaces or the places never seen …
Although the ways and means are there by ship or train or plane,there
are restraints like cash that may too often make us stay
at home and dream.

* * *

The possibilities of travel can be ultimately endless …
How did Holst conceive his sonic journeys into Planetary Space,
long before those powerful rockets made the early voyages possible?
He surely had the gift to free the rich imagination of his mind,
to explore those places well beyond the reach of material restraint.

* * *

While visiting St. Petersburg, I met a Russian Psychotherapist,
who claimed he had discovered & practised psycho-energetic ways
to deflect rockets or torpedoes …

Hearing of this, the Russian Navy invited him to do some tests,
and when these proved successful, they employed him to join
a nuclear submarine as part of the torpedo defence crew.
He calls this the science of Psychotronics, and there is now a Psychotronics
Organisation for research, practice and collaboration.

*   *   *

(This idea continued in "The Travelling Mind" poem)

The Mechanisation of Time

Since the invention of the early mechanical clocks.
Like one Waterclock in Exeter Cathedral dated 1284,
and their Astronomical clock (15), with its moon phases,
these clever devices have increasingly ruled our lives …
No doubt what came before were sundials,
side really errant, but useful to devoted Parishioners & Sailors.

*   *   *

These seasoned men and women knew the progress of time
found within their minds and bodies
so what need had they for knowing 12 divisions of the day?
The answer might be found in Sacred Geometry,
that twelve is somehow built into the structure of our brains,
and thus becomes a natural rhythm in our daily lives …
Sacred Geometry is also related to Earths axial rotations and traverse round the Sun.

*   *   *

How would the Navigators know where to go
without their clock and compass?
The watch is a wonderful invention,
but time watching has become too much the ruler of our daily lives.

*   *   *

Perhaps the Hogi Tribe in the Andes had it right,
to ban the use of clocks and watches in their Country,
as their way to stop the onset of Techno-Society;
Being a small tribe enables this, while larger countries
are so bound up in precisely timed events, would find it
difficult to do without their clocks and electronic pace makers.

*   *   *

Why do we love our time scarce life,
when living in one's mindful moment,
as my Buddhist training says, can bring the joy
in blissful consciousness.
Dear reader, I do confess I mostly live outside the moment.

*   *   *

Time Past

Memory is like the black cat on a pitch dark night,
It may be illusive, may be fantastic, may seem surreal
or exciting, to become the stuff of legends, old stories round a fireside.

*   *   *

Our memories do slowly fade, like golden leaves in setting suns.
We remember to share what we like to remember,
and to forget what causes pain, -
in one's mind of 10 million leaves, only one hopes the best remain.
The tyranny of time lets others fall away,
not to be caught before they fall into oblivion.

*   *   *

We love to tell our stories to our friends and
often find the art is in embellishment;
Great the raconteur who scoops a silver fish
within this still and quite pool of consciousness,
to build a tale of mystery and magic,
that's each time heard afresh to send the listening minds
into a reverie.

*   *   *

When end is near, the record of one's life is played
like contents of a computer hard-drive,
all life's experiences, relationships, accidents, joys, & landscapes,
the brain remembers all, nothing's lost …
One hoped the best of this is kept within the soul,
to move into the tunnel to another world,
where there may be the answers to the mystery of Life?

*   *   *

Perhaps the past is now, for time is surely cyclic,
like the snake swallowing its tail …
Even the ancient prophets foretold Einstein's Space Time Continuum,
That time depends on Space that is forever all around us.
It seems that Time dilates to match the quality of experience and perception.

*   *   *

Dark Times ~ After the Flood

12th Dec. 2006
Revised Sept. 2008

Who can see the icecaps melting,
and the seas steady rise,
under a heady rain of consumables,
fogging the night bright Cosmos,
in the lost city where soon it's million lights submerge,
great generators fall silent, their primal energies lost,
under the flood.

*   *   *

Who can hear the crackling ice falling into distant oceans,
when their ears are plugged with electronica?
Who can turn their eyes upwards to majestic heavens,
to see the ever-changing chromatic harmonies,
soundscapes & symphonies waiting to be enjoyed.

*   *   *

Build your ships while you can,
to voyage the greater lake
beyond the golden gate of your dreams,
into the spacious higher hills and mountains,
swept clean by recent raging storms,
the new lakes overspilling into streams falling
to the vast seas merging into the sky.

*   *   *

Welcome return you dear roots,
dare to climb the great tree of your destiny,
into the simplicity of life embraced & loved
by the ultimate web of your planetary nature.

*   *   *

Enter the luxury of an uncluttered existence,
a barefoot dance in the hills wild meadows,
drink deep the intimacy of love around you.
To merge your mind & soul into its warmth.

   * * *

Can you see the ice caps melting
and the seas steady rising?
Do you fear the loss of technological routine,
or welcome a simpler life,
a return to your heart and soul's true home.

   * * *

<u>Tewkesbury under Flood, August 2007</u>. *This depicts my conjectural view over the flooded River Severn towards Tewkesbury Town with its splendid Abbey. It shows a family descending a lane from hills on the Welsh Marches side of this great River. The exceptional rains of that year caused widespread flooding in England, and I was reminded of a novel by the great 19th century writer, Richard Jefferies, called After London, about England reverting to a simpler life when the main riverside Cities were destroyed under floods. It's a salutary reminder of what could happen with radical climate change when rises in sea levels combine with flooding.*

Life is the Mind of this Universe

Nightly I love to walk under a purple vault,
scored by ten thousand million diamonds slowly rotating…
how can I project my being into the mind of this,
our homespun Universe…?

*   *   *

When time is right will mind collapse to free my soul
into this ultimate so spacious unity,
or can my soulful will transport me to another state of being,
to find another home to grow inside?

*   *   *

While walking face upturned, this is my view into this vastly
brain-like web, wondering, will this just guide me to oblivion,
or to another voyage across this endless space,
to find the ultimate mystery of Life.

*   *   *

One fact is sure, that life itself continues…
it just rotates, as do the planets round the sun,
for me there cannot be oblivion, since life renews itself eternally,
and this so finely colour filled arcadia we call Nature,
can herself migrate to many other levels, unknown, unseen,
then this fair Earth would slowly fade with all its beings too!

*   *   *

Everyone would like to know,
just what does happen when we go?
Could it be our souls migrate into a different place?
When we could choose instead to fly into the realm of lightless space.

*   *   *

Though ideas are endless, this one is very clear -
our bodies age as do all beings, & then we fear to lose our personality,
our sensual pleasures, creative powers, friends, lovers,
and all the beauties of Nature…
perhaps our greatest fear of all is not to be at all!

*   *   *

Considering all, it seems one gets the truest insight
to another life, within the theatre of our dreams,
the door to that vast realm called Consciousness.

*   *   *

Love that Makes the Man (Birth of Friendship)

'26th & 27th Feb. 2013
(Updated 2015)

This new-born man received no rules
for loving woman, but etched so deeply in his heart,
the latent instinct soon emerged…

*   *   *

Come twenty years, began his wandering search,
across the beautiful world to find,
to meet his dream shaped spiritual lover,
in distant Countries far & wide,
armed with a faultless guide called Faith in Life,
must one enlightened day,
drive his skeptic mind to lose its way,
abandon preconceptions, listening instead
to the soulful song of a heart,
too long ensnared by his ever restless mind.

*   *   *

Yes, just now you know you've sought in vain,
till realisation came, this cannot be the way,
just give your mind a holiday,
let soul take the helm,
and consciousness will find your true love.

*   *   *

Relax, watch, listen by every means,
perceive in Nature all around, the deeper wisdoms.
When this skill becomes a habit,
then you'll quickly know the love you need
is not out there, but here inside you.

*   *   *

Sequoia

Written under this great tree at
Gaunts House, Dorset in 2010

Tree, do you see me?
Me, the insignificant transient,
you, the great and powerful tree,
will endure such varied seasons,
for many long years, and many generations.

* * *

In you I hear a powerful symphony,
your trunk the grounded bass continuum
your branches swooping downwards
forming complex counterpoints and fugues.

* * *

Now I stroke your aromatic fronds
hoping to evoke a sensual song…
here to me this tree speaks its ancient legends,
when the raging storms have played it
like a mighty harp, and when
the flashes crackled all about its crown.

* * *

Many searing dramas have you seen played out
within the solid walls of this great house
the chattering voices of the Balls,
or lonely ballads of the Troubadour.

* * *

The warmest tones of wrinkled bark & deep green falls,
do radiate their song across the park
caressing many other trees & rhythms
to gather complex harmonies.

* * *

These stories I'm now hearing in these gorgeous sounds
are overlays descending in this tumbledown,
time is gathered, then time is given away,
I can learn your stately generosity,
and just by drawing up the depths,
you forge this blessed alchemy,
You give to all who need, including me.

*   *   *

The Crystal Pool (Part 2 of The Primal Splash)

You are the precious crystal
cast into the pool of Life,
and this stone lodges in your heart,
from whence the ripples emanate
in circles all around wher'ere you roam.

*   *   *

Let your heart shaped crystal
radiate the love to all about you,
then all these living beings
will feel your blessed presence
so then will glow, as does the gem itself!

*   *   *

These beings you meet
can said to be the points upon your circle,
that when traversed across in harmonic resonance
will form a sacred mandala,
whose centre forms the essence of your soul.

*   *   *

NB. This poem was mostly inspired by Part 1: "The Primal Splash", but my recent readings about Islamic Philosophy by Tom Bree (in "The Chalice" P.10 Summer 2015) prompted these extra lines as Part 2.

The Gift of Gardens

If you want to find the inner peace of your true self,
then wander into a quiet well-tended garden,
where aromatic herbs and flowers grace the air…
such gardens are the best of earthly gifts.

*　　*　　*

If you feel stressed and worried in this frenetic world,
try sitting in your garden or the local park,
on a warm spring or summer day,
when scents of Nature will come to hold your hands,
and the atmospheric humming sounds around will soothe
your mind and heart.

*　　*　　*

My friends the Jains have always said to me:~
"Enter our garden here
and let Mother Earth just take you for a walk.
Let her heal your troubled soul,
and let her green heart return you to the balance
that you surely crave."

*　　*　　*

For here in this special garden
you can save yourself, sitting peacefully in meditation…
let this garden enfold you in a warmly scented embrace,
for she has a natural passion to heal, calm & restore
like no other. For this while, let your busy thoughts
fall away, so Nature's power can move in.

*　　*　　*

The Myth of Separation

Is this just another illusion, this gender difference?
Like that of separation from our Mother Earth.
Why do we so glorify our parts apart,
our precious ego-worth?

*   *   *

Then you say: "I've spent half my life
nurturing my character and my ego,
so why should I now throw it all away,
and say, it's all illusion!"

*   *   *

Then comes the mystery called Love,
that sings inside your cage,
a powerful lyric:~
"set me free, set me free!"

*   *   *

So this love becomes the liberator,
the powerful Angel to destroy your ego…
if wise you let it have its sway,
to lead you swimming into unity with Life today.

*   *   *

NB. Sun. Oct 29th 2017:~ Today the clocks go back 1 hour. If time went back too, it might be very interesting? Perhaps I can write a story about "When time went back"? It might be that everyone would miss out their last hour completely, then I wonder where one would go? To what place, what happenings, heaven or hell? I can ask the audience for answers to this?

The Primal Splash

18th July 2012
Minor revisions; June 2014

Casting a stone into a still millpond,
filled with wonder how these ripples radiate
such perfect circles from this alien energy,
thrusting its heavy shock into this limpid silence.

*   *   *

No angry reaction, instead a passionate embrace,
and the perfect feminine response saying:~
"you break my beauty-filled repose,
but still, be still in me my love,
as welcome I your company & rugged woes."

*   *   *

May have I this heavy heart, a heart of stone,
but when I dive into your enfolding spring,
can feel my searing problems fall away
and rising weightless great the warmth
of sunlight in this newborn day.

*   *   *

So now may I just thank you pool,
and you too sunlight,
who always give your healing powers
without restraint or call for thanks,
for your clear waters spring,
from this the very rocky womb of our fair earth.

*   *   *

Your feedback please

Contact me on tel. 01803 866349 (pref); or *jeffrey@worldpeacegardensnet.org*

Printed in the United States
By Bookmasters